Cool Sugar Skull Coloring Book for Adults

BONJOUR PRINTABLES

COPYRIGHT 2020 BONJOUR PRINTABLES
ALL RIGHTS RESERVED

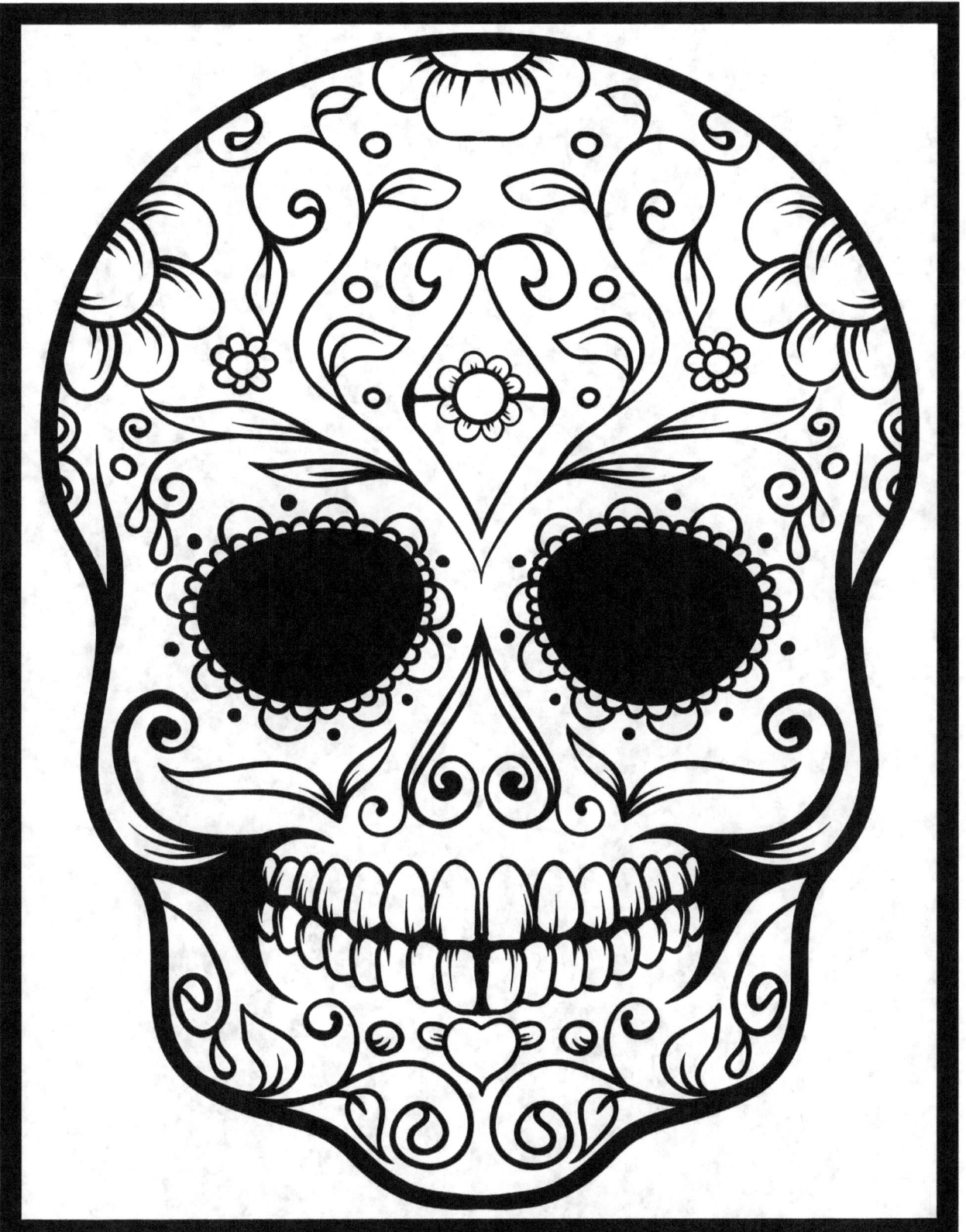

Sugar Skull 1
BONJOUR PRINTABLES

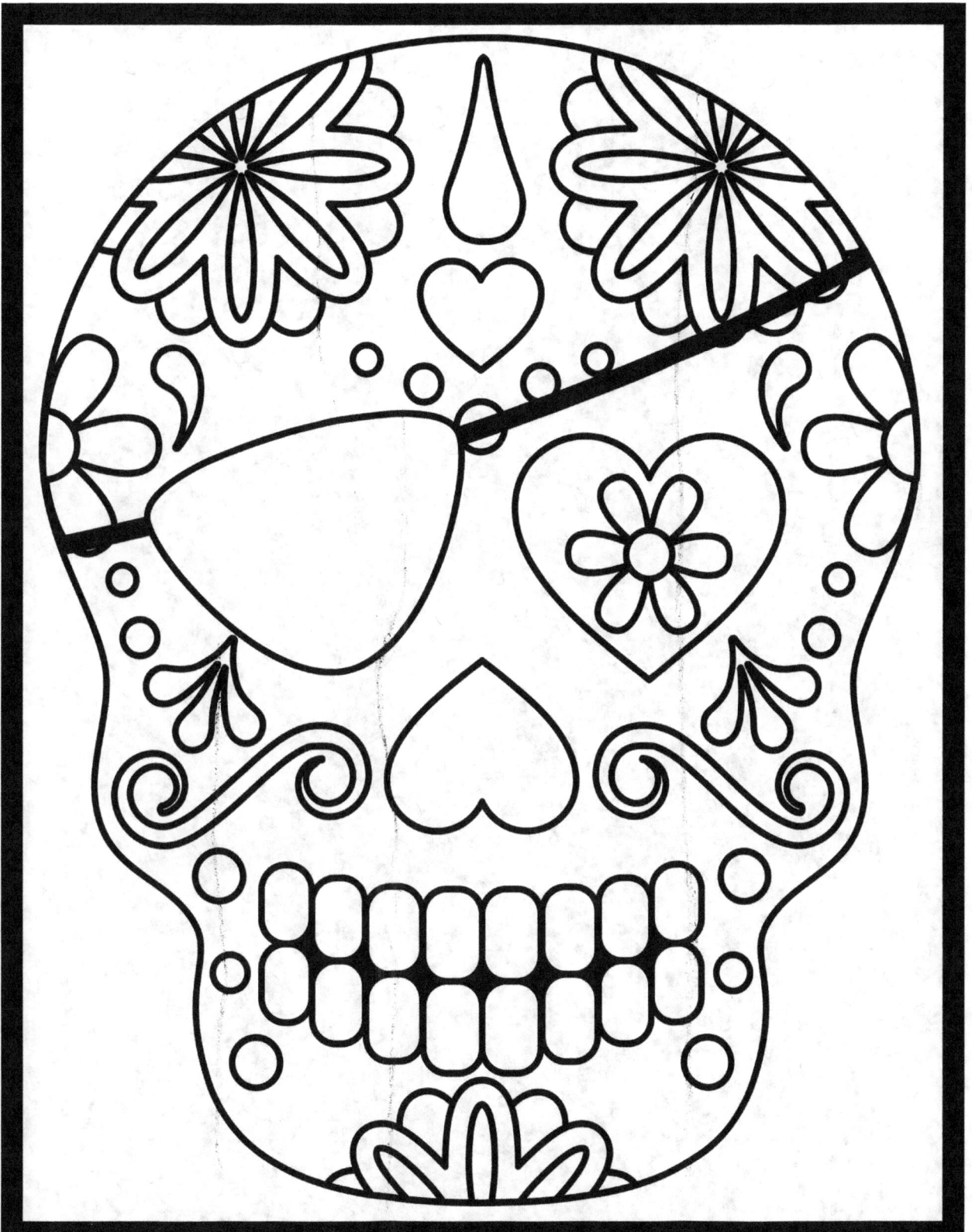

Sugar Skull 2
BONJOUR PRINTABLES

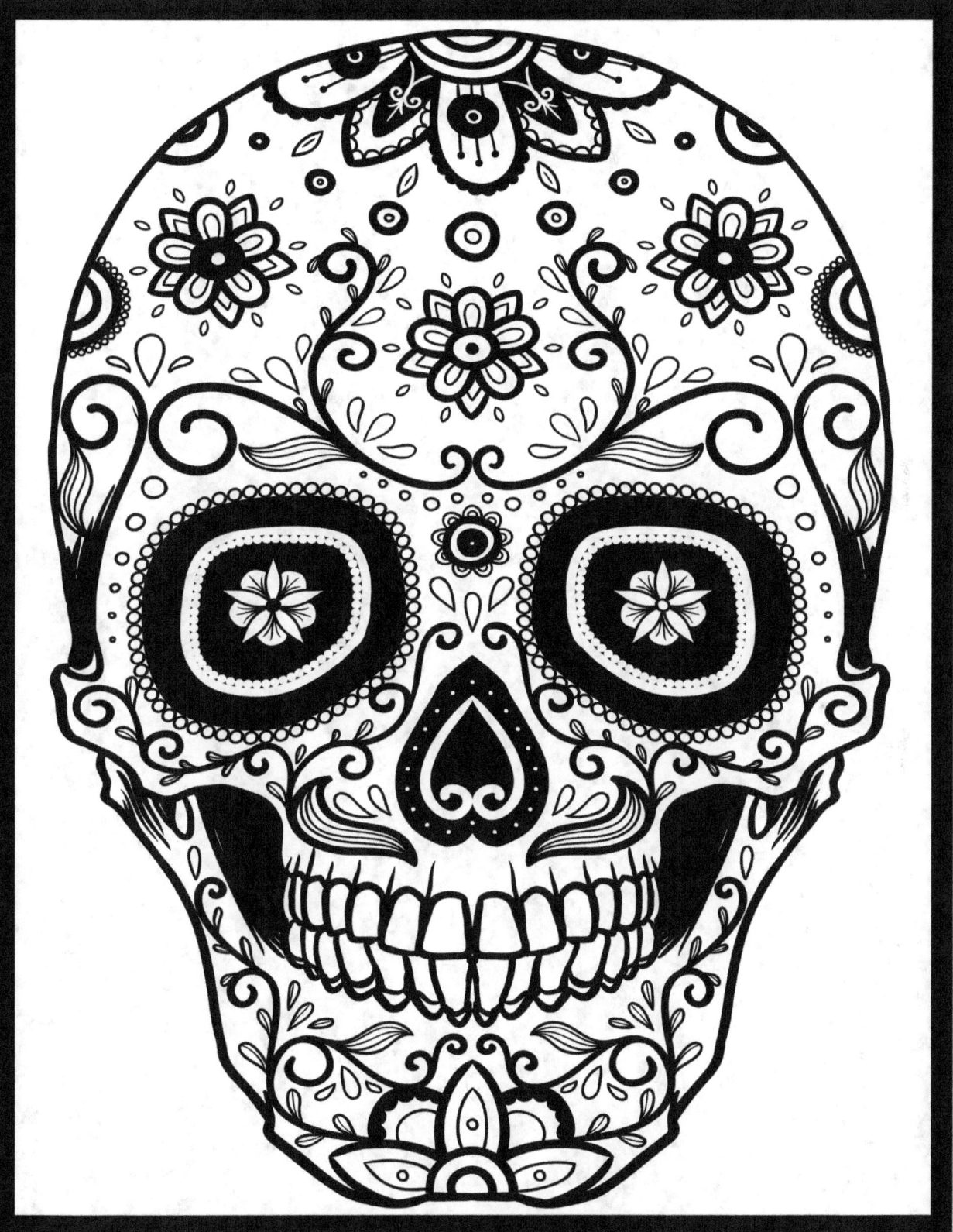

Sugar Skull 3
BONJOUR PRINTABLES

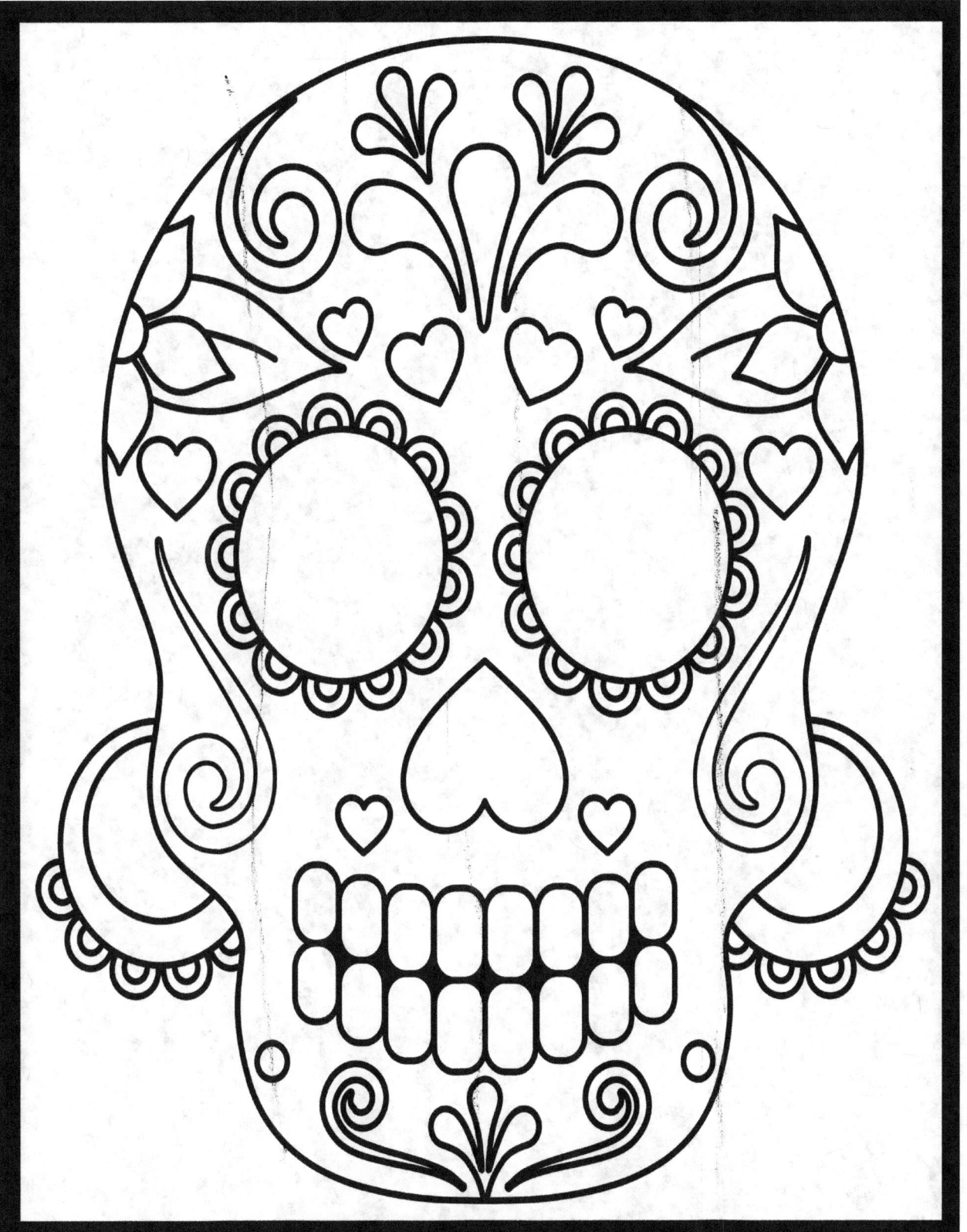

Sugar Skull 4
BONJOUR PRINTABLES

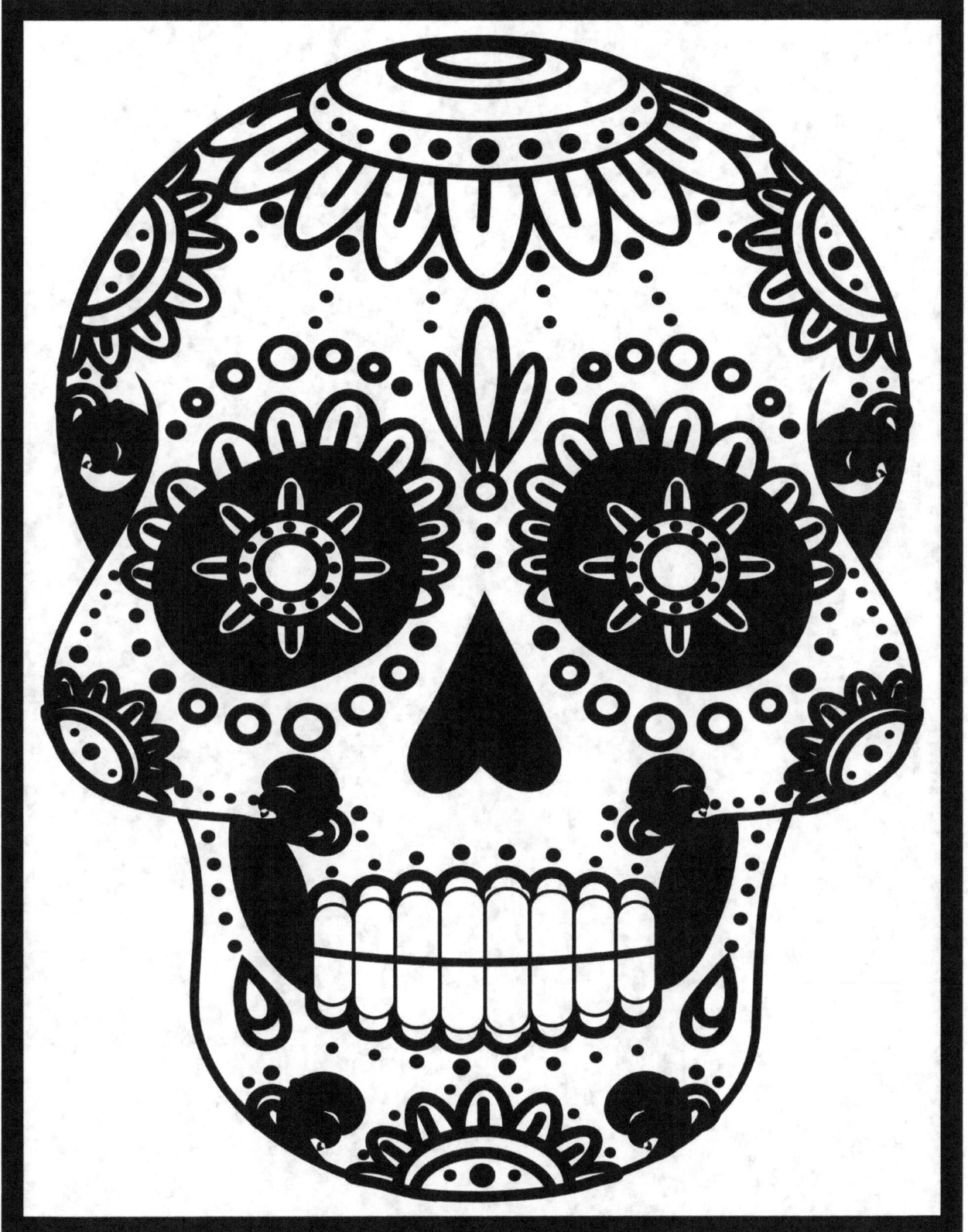

Sugar Skull 5
BONJOUR PRINTABLES

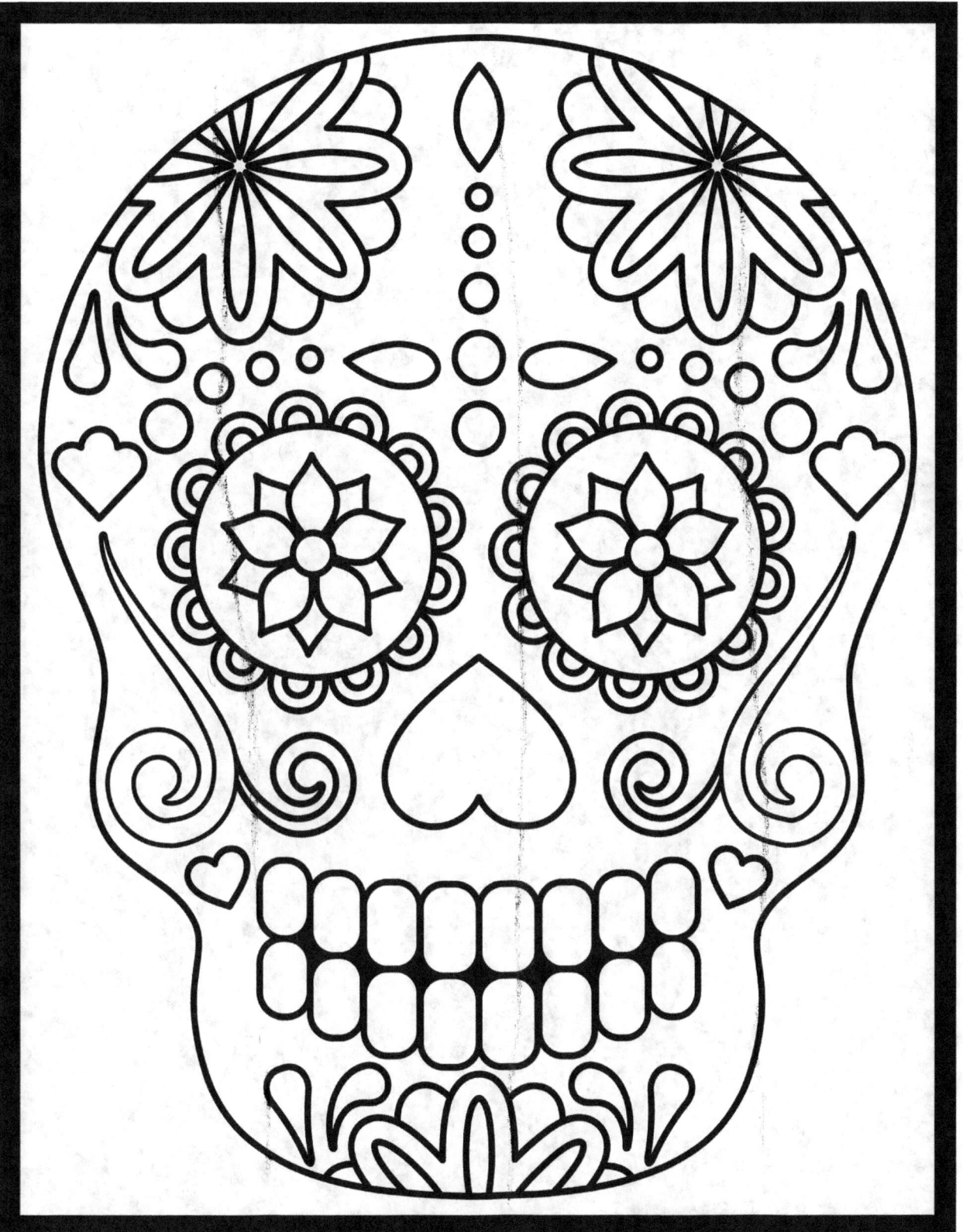

Sugar Skull 6
BONJOUR PRINTABLES

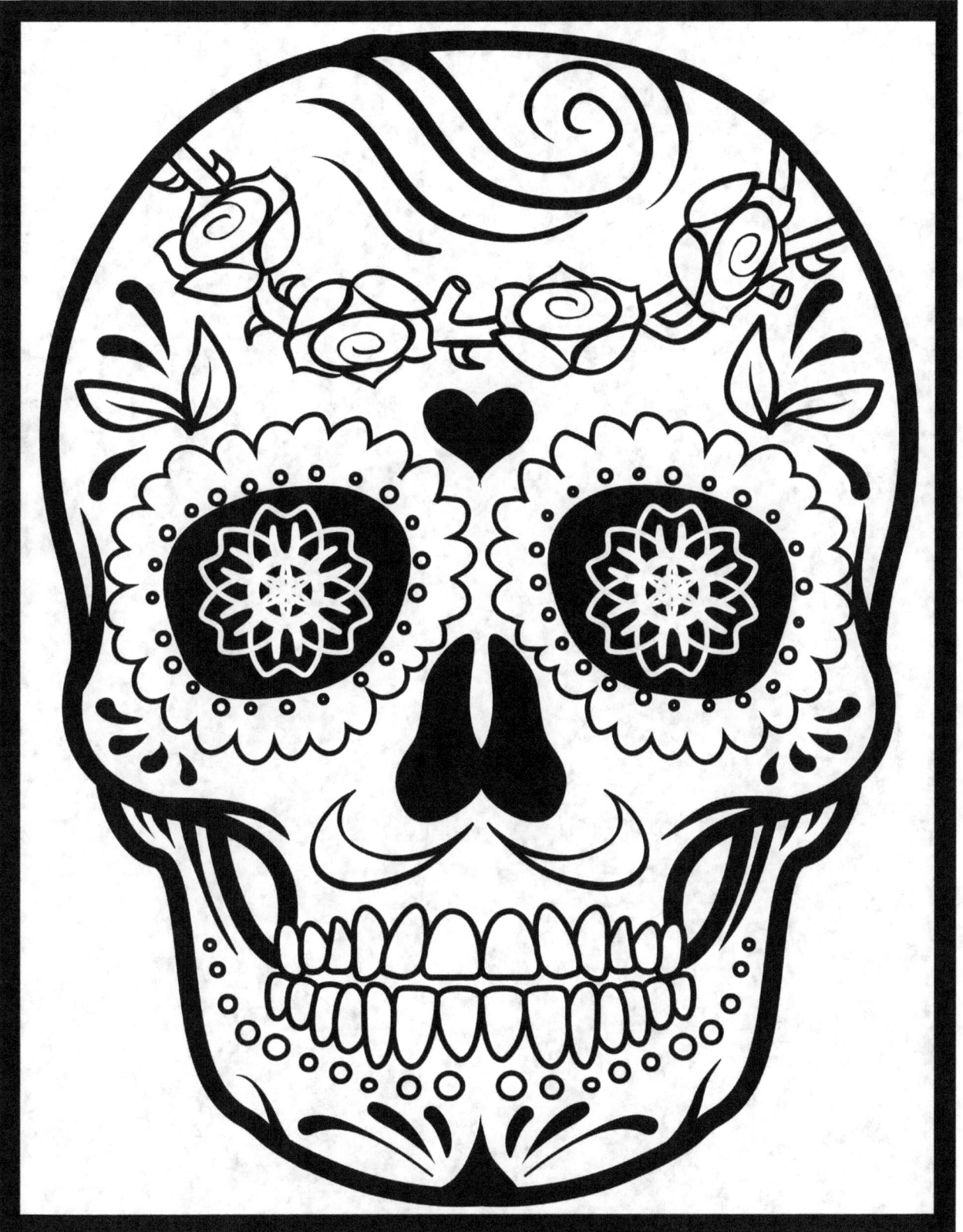

Sugar Skull 7
BONJOUR PRINTABLES

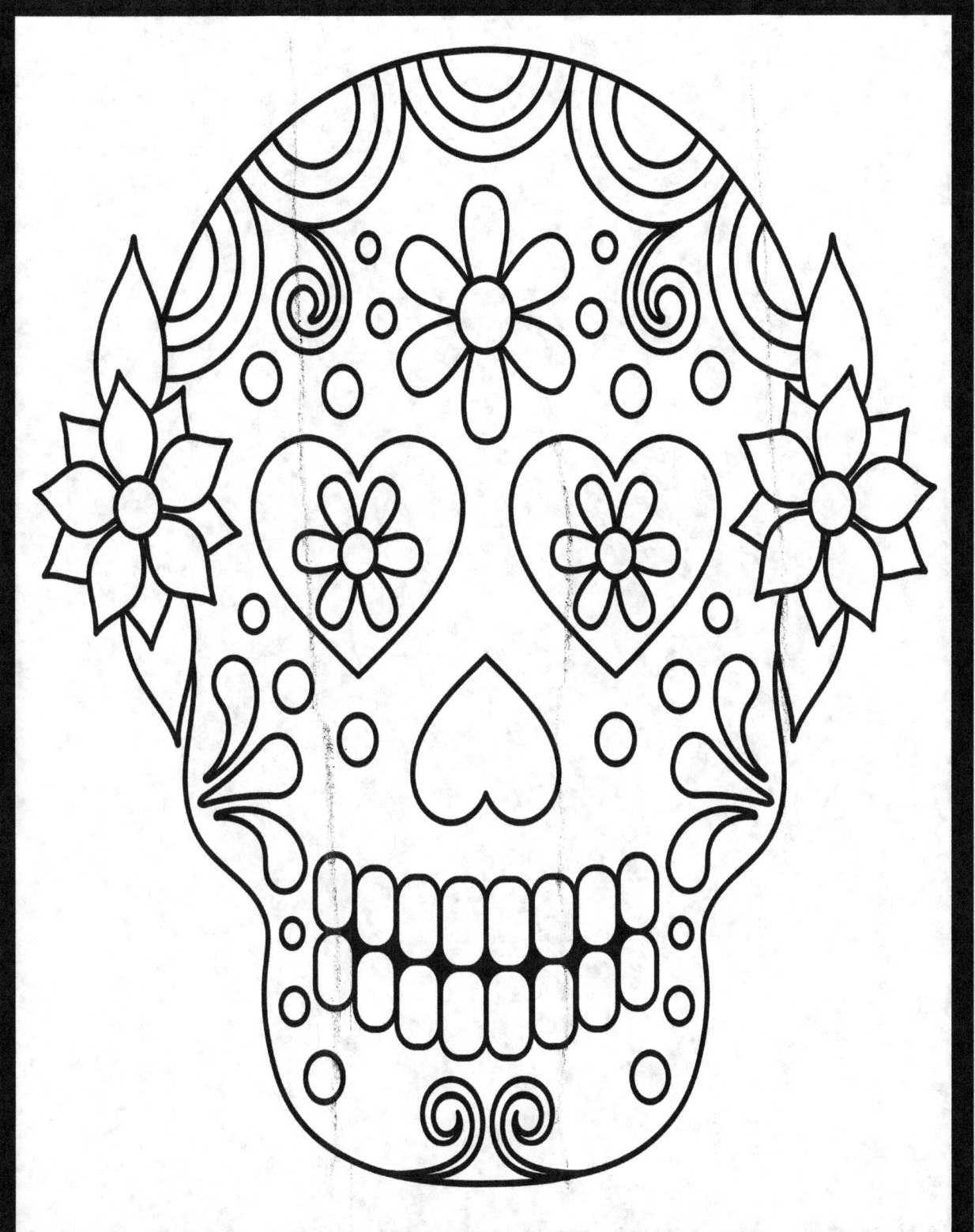

Sugar Skull 8
BONJOUR PRINTABLES

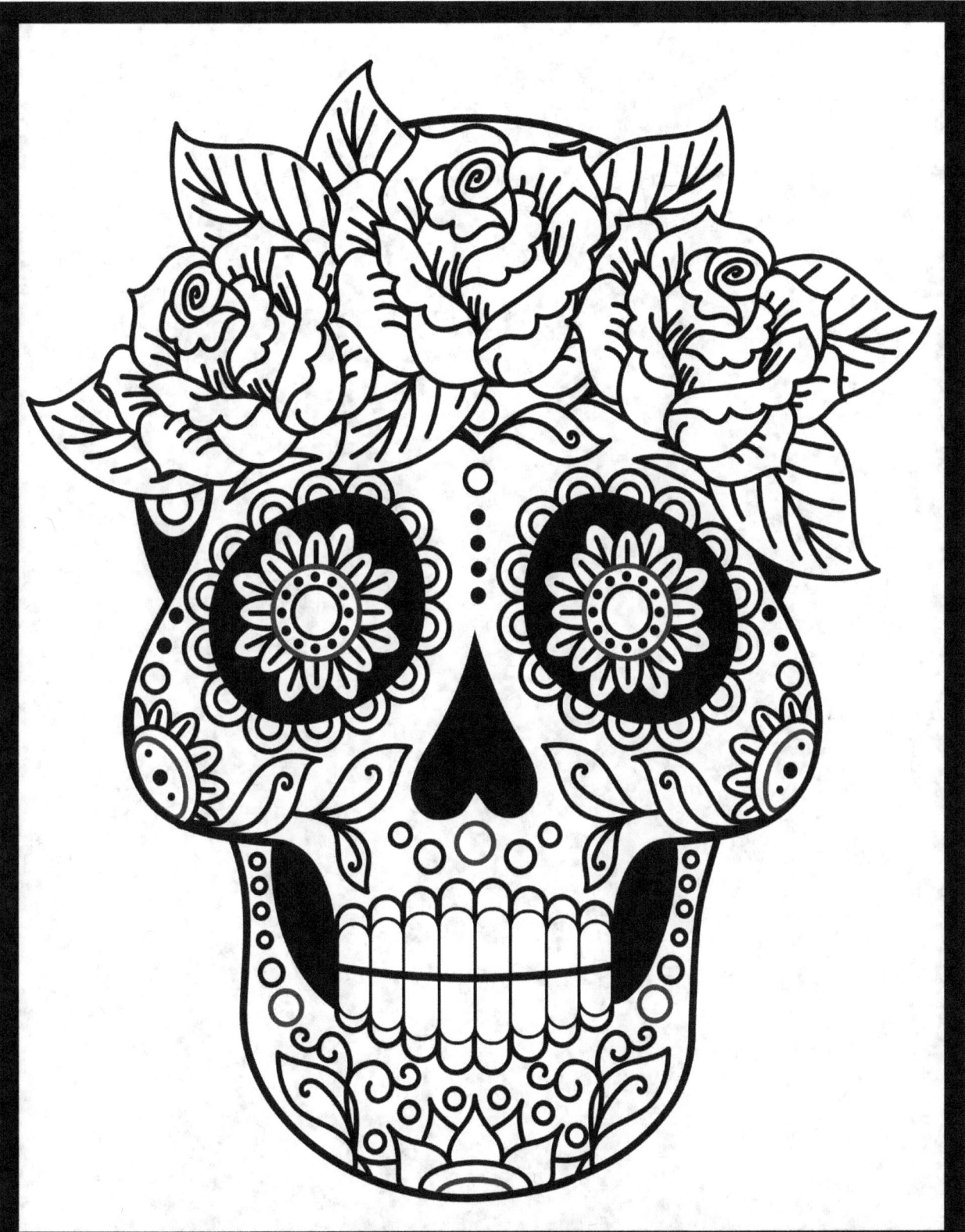

Sugar Skull 9
BONJOUR PRINTABLES

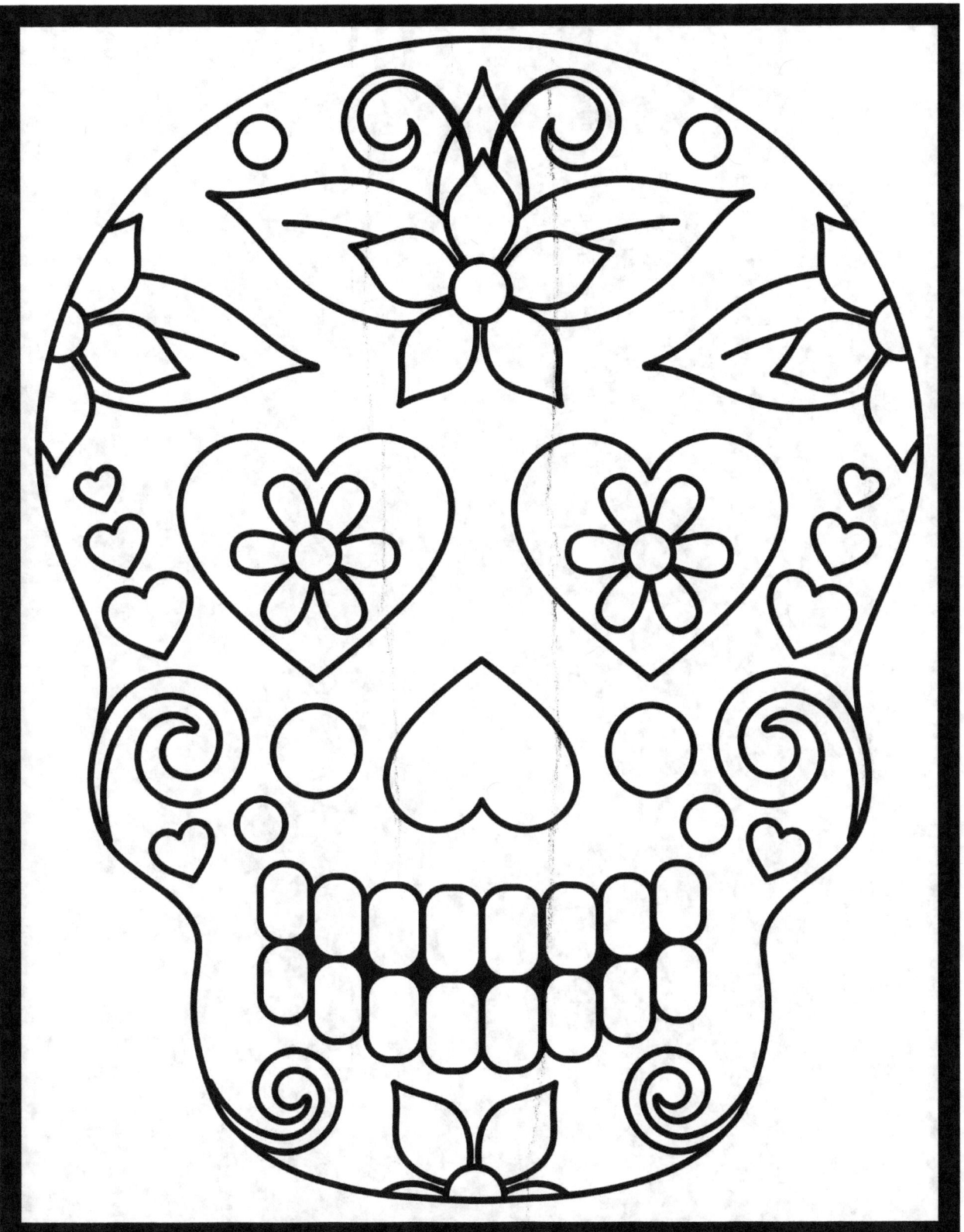

Sugar Skull 10
BONJOUR PRINTABLES

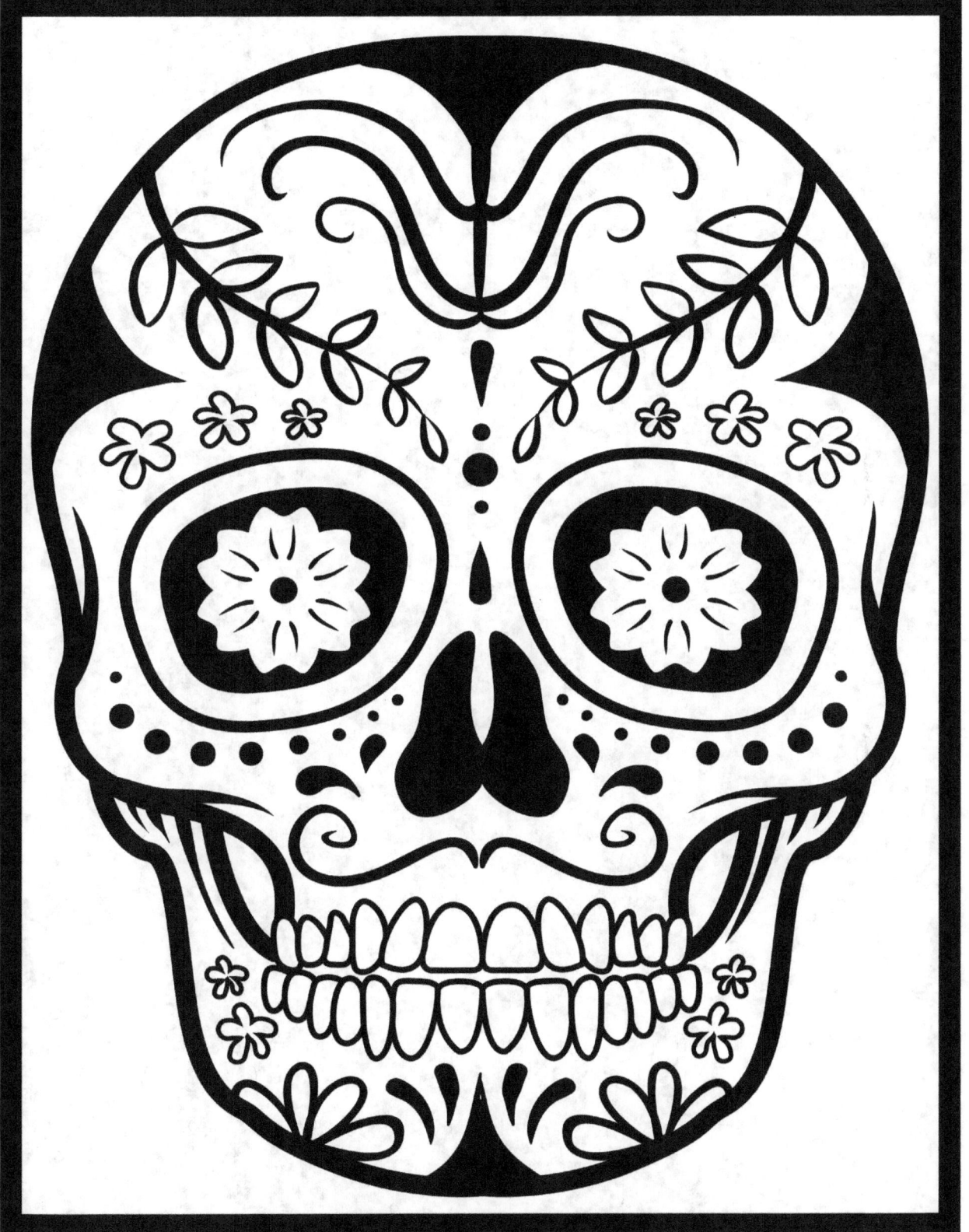

Sugar Skull 11
BONJOUR PRINTABLES

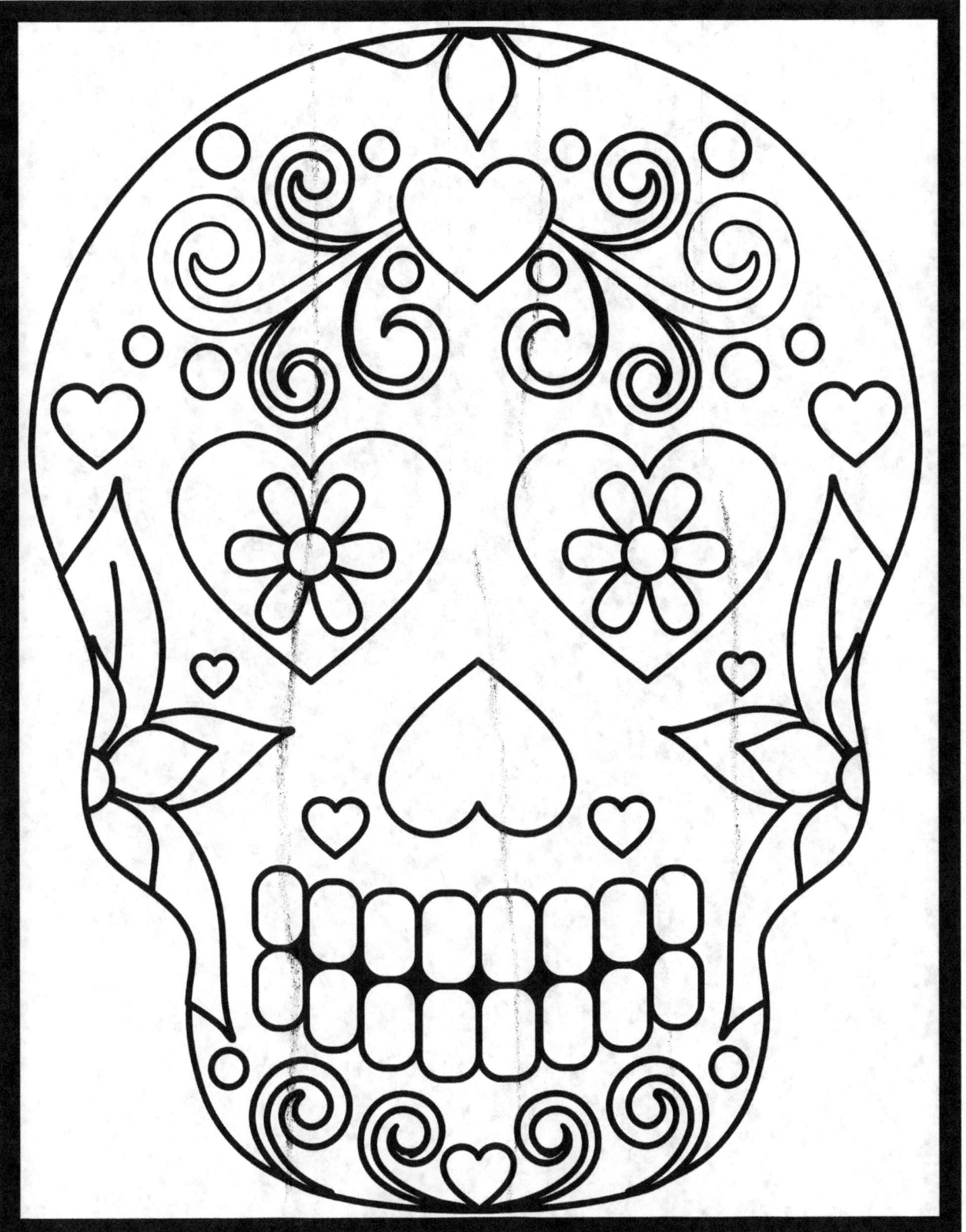

Sugar Skull 12

BONJOUR PRINTABLES

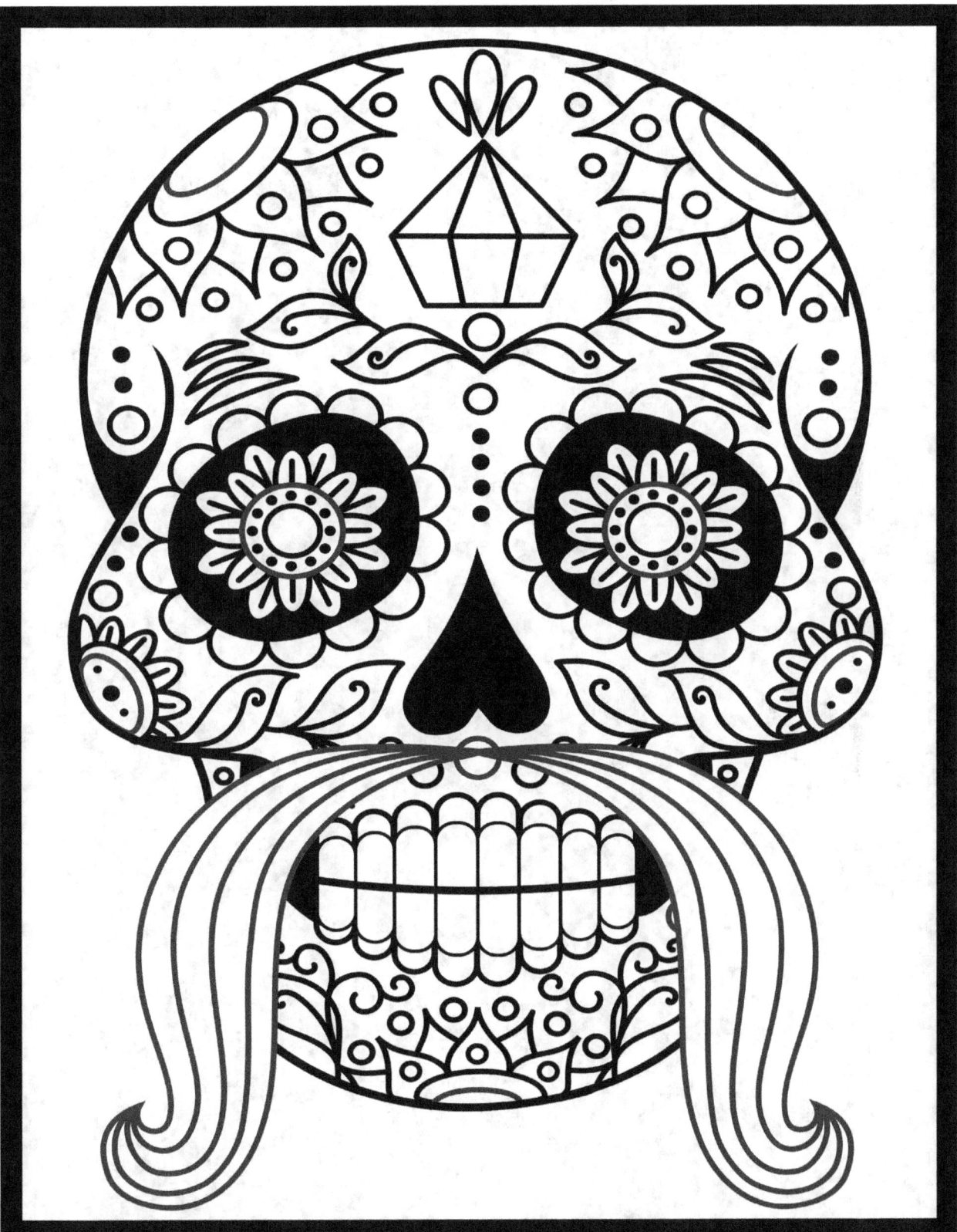

Sugar Skull 13
BONJOUR PRINTABLES

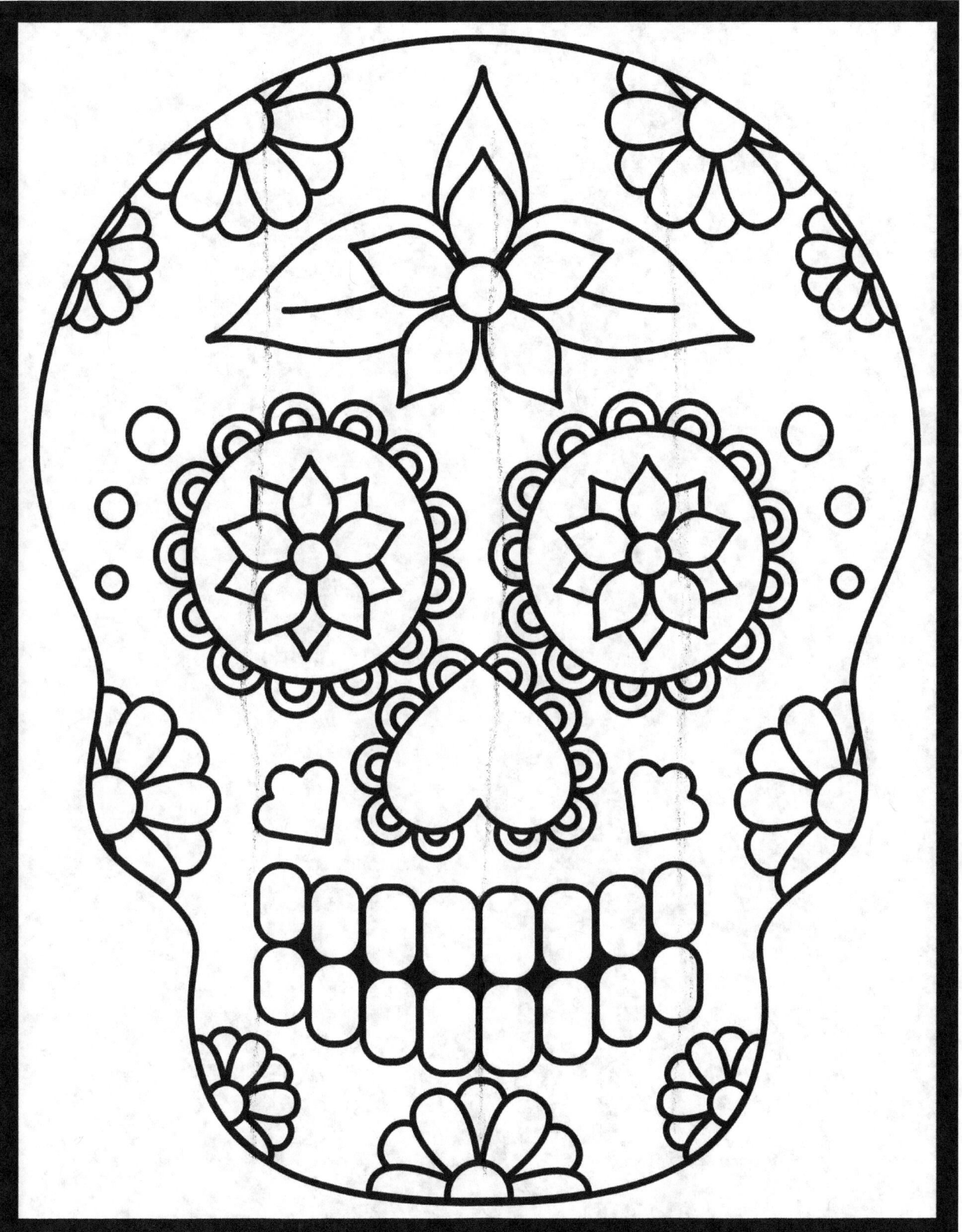

Sugar Skull 14
BONJOUR PRINTABLES

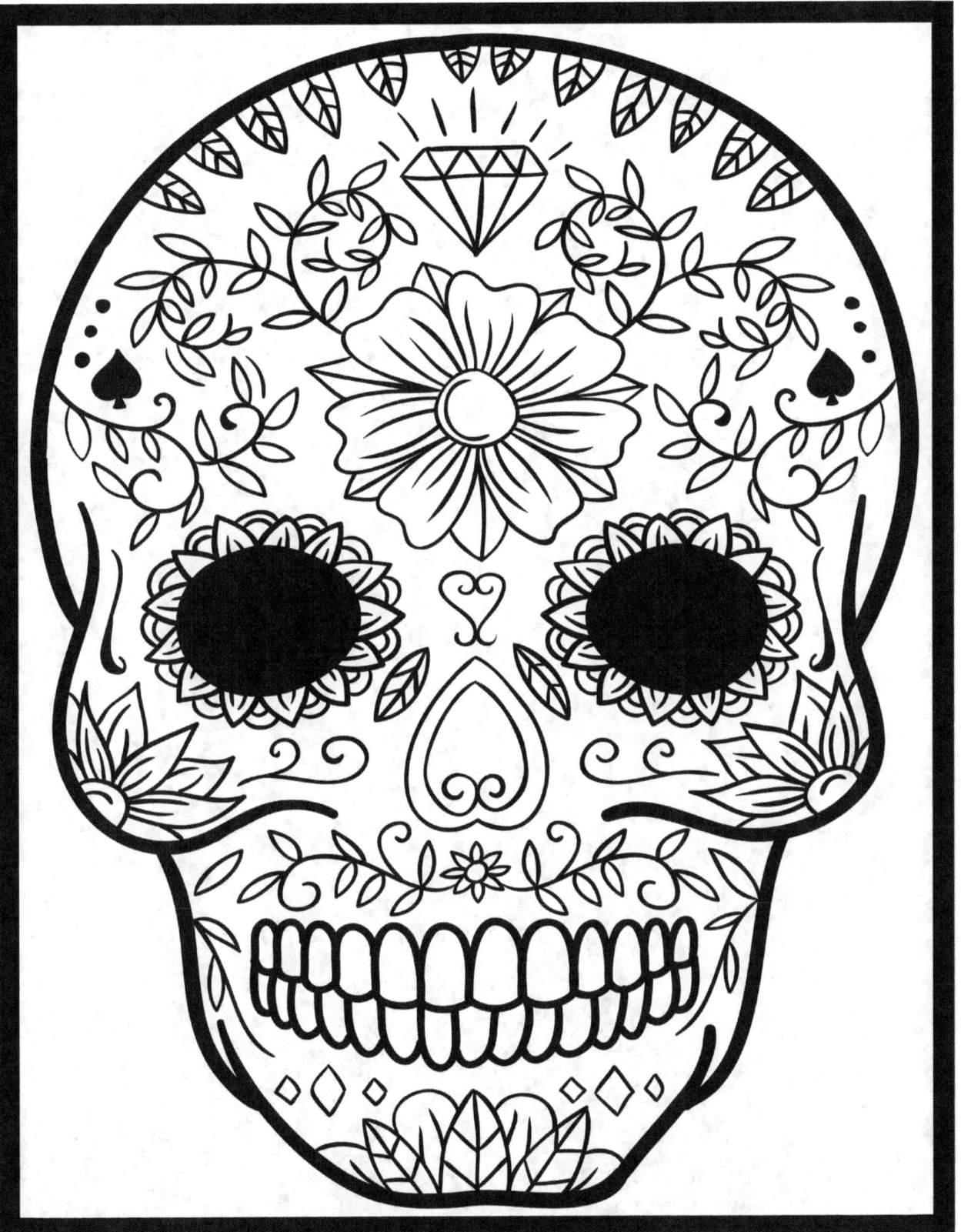

Sugar Skull 15
BONJOUR PRINTABLES

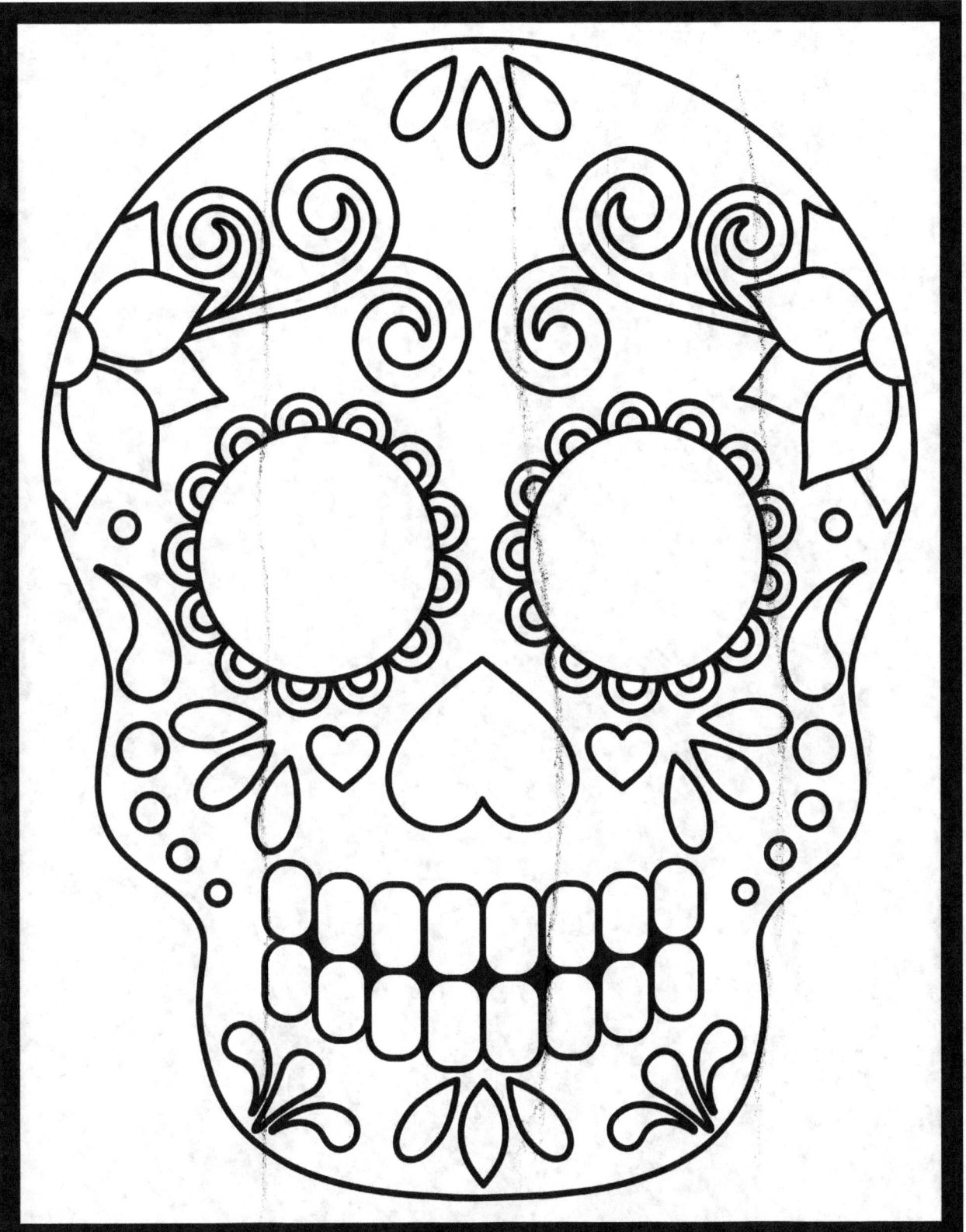

Sugar Skull 16
BONJOUR PRINTABLES

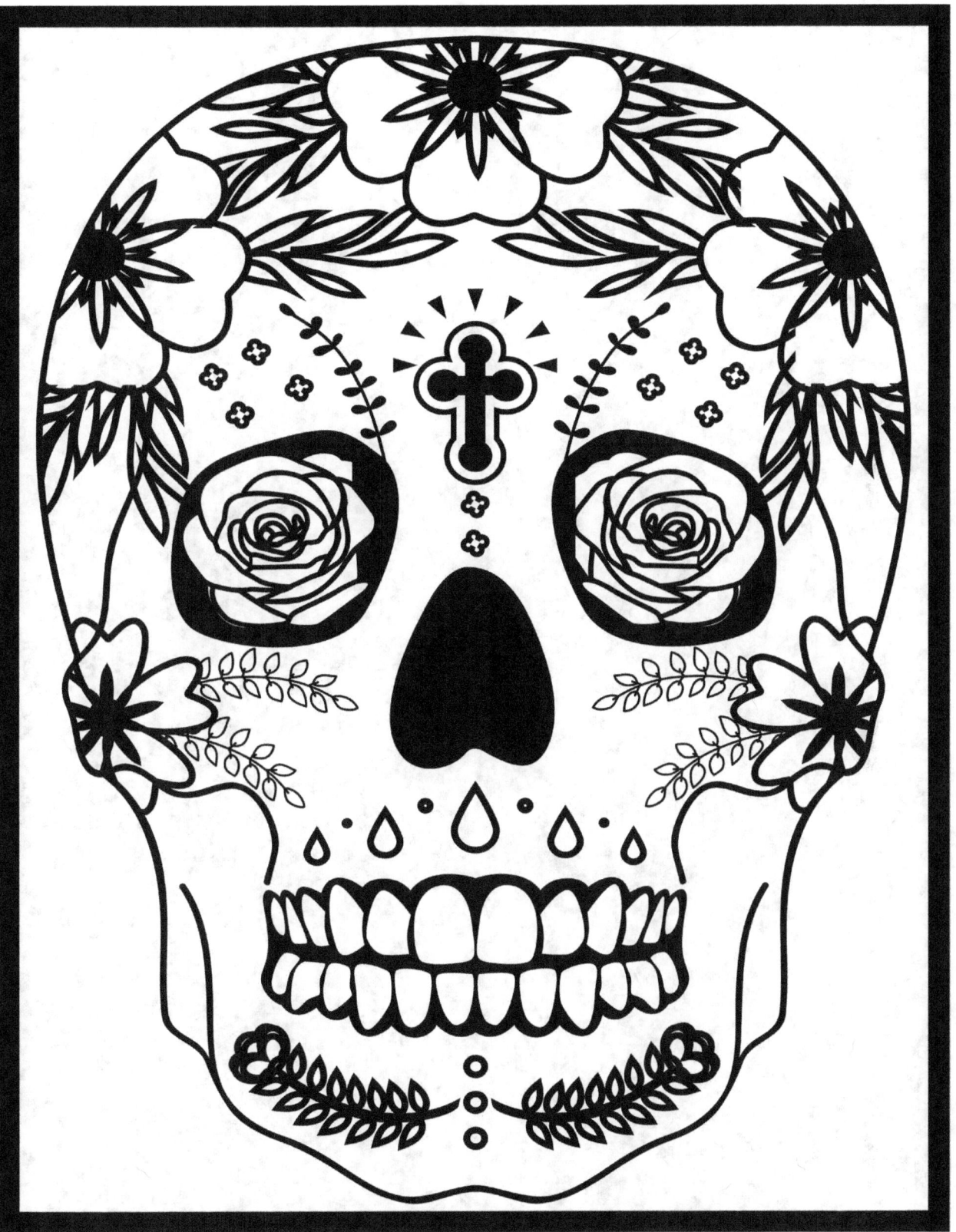

Sugar Skull 17
BONJOUR PRINTABLES

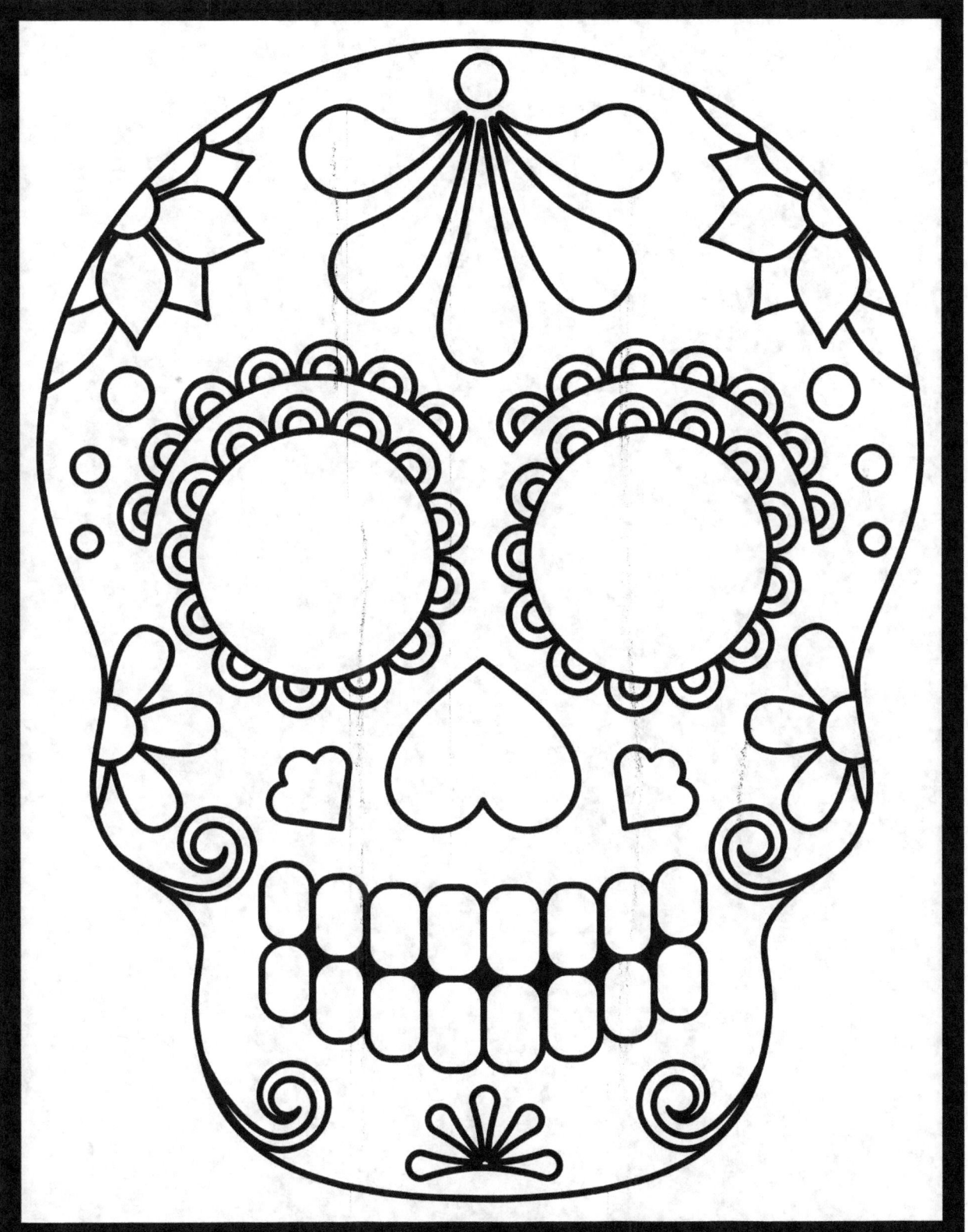

Sugar Skull 18

BONJOUR PRINTABLES

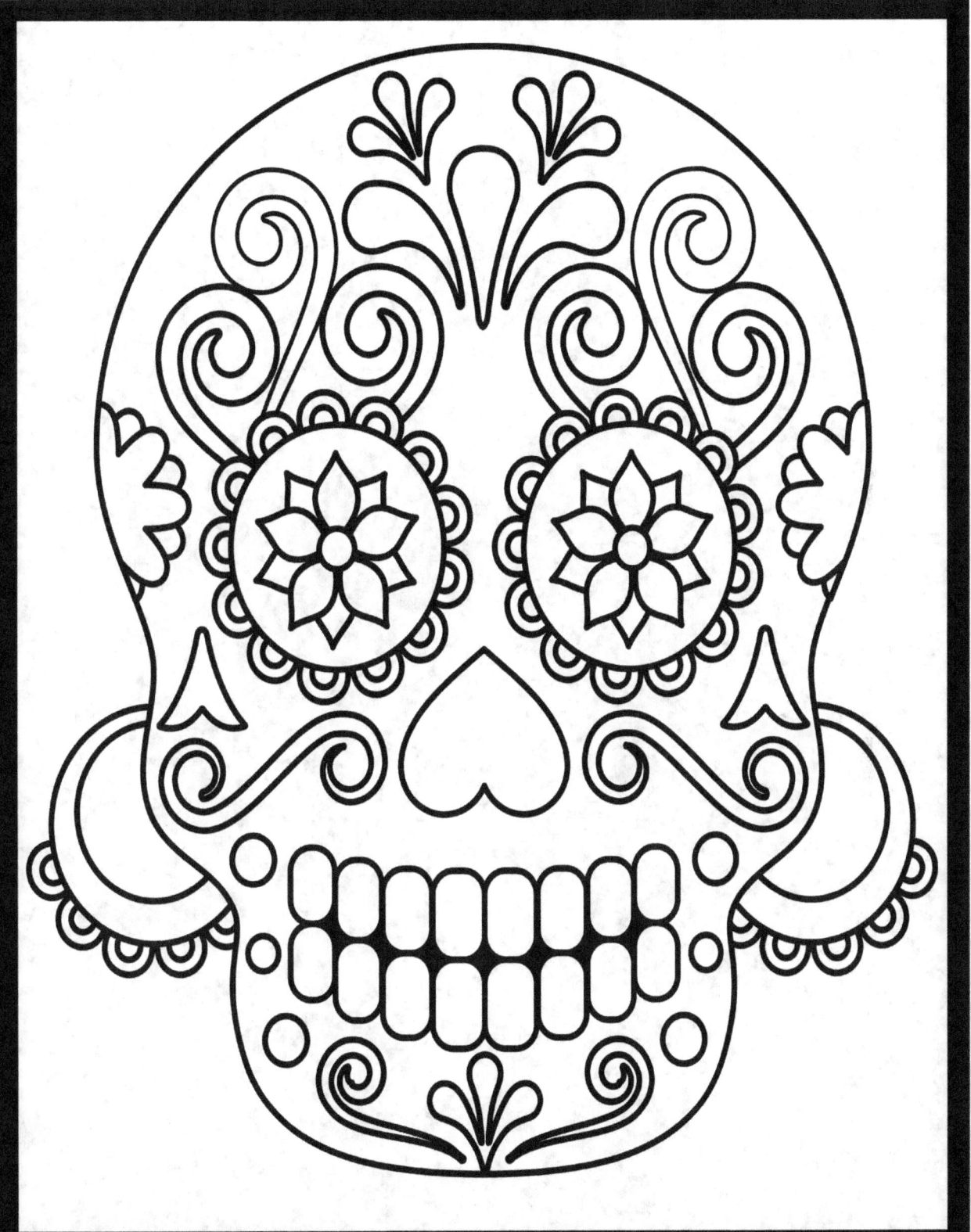

Sugar Skull 19
BONJOUR PRINTABLES

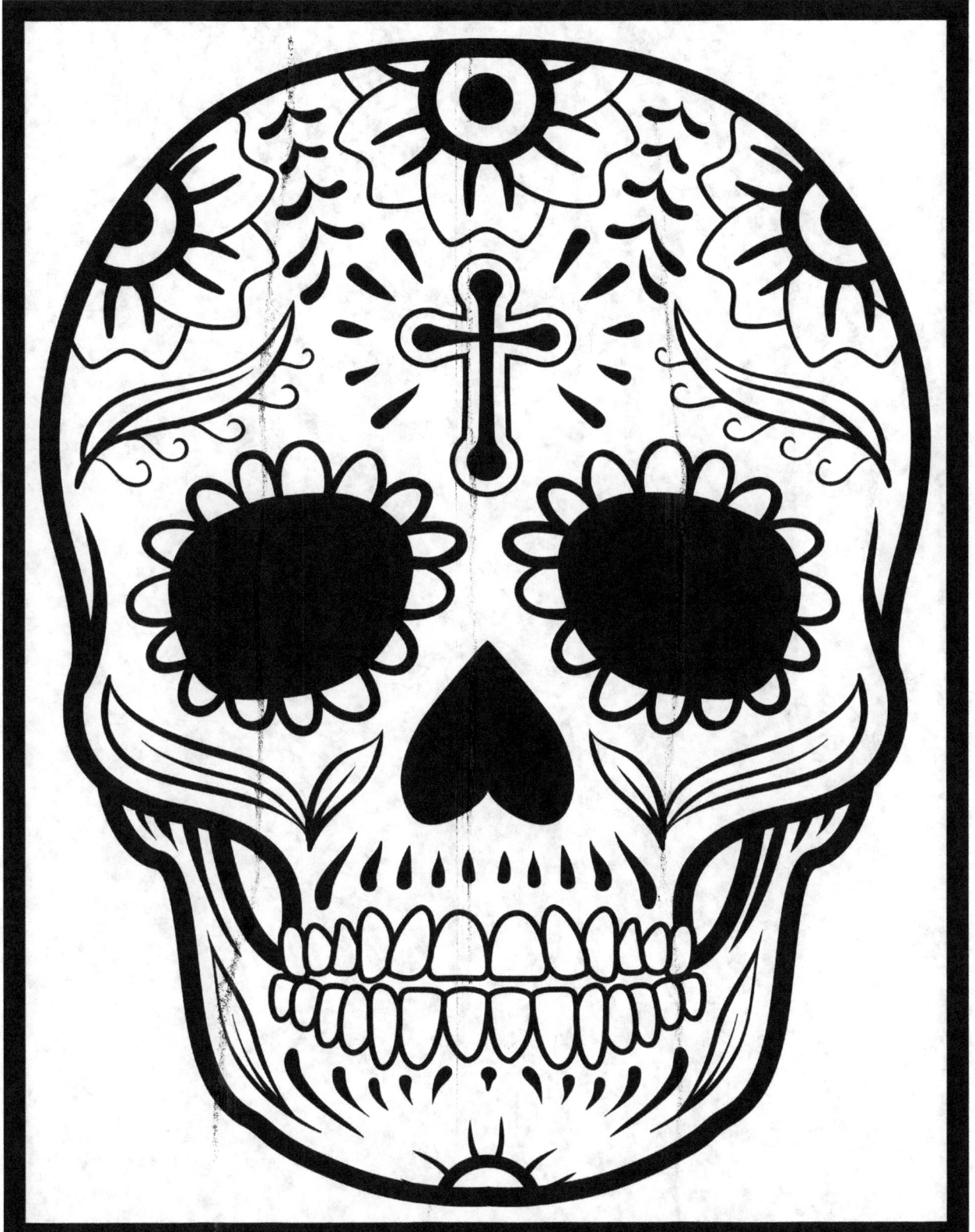

Sugar Skull 20
BONJOUR PRINTABLES

Sugar Skull 20
BONJOUR PRINTABLES

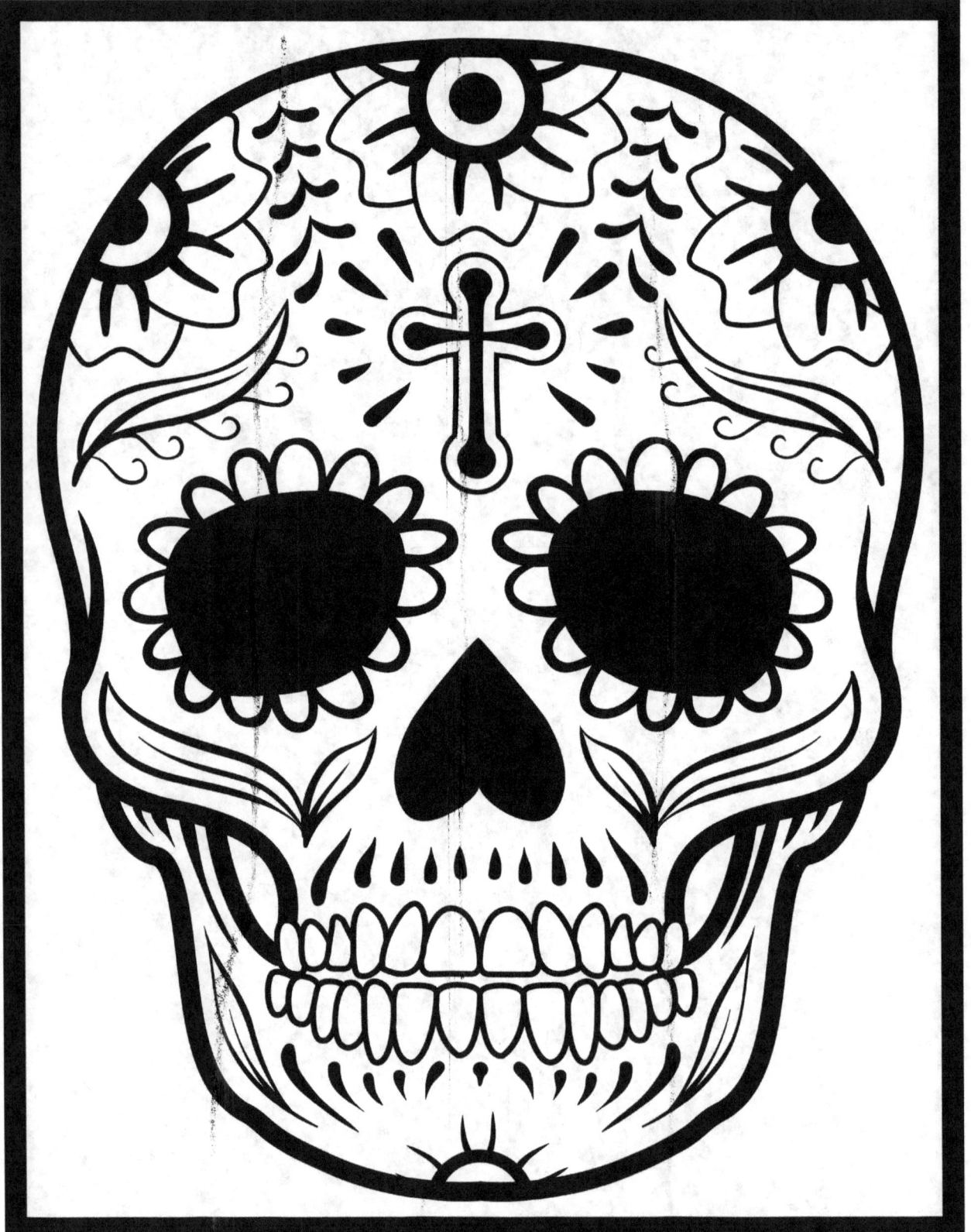

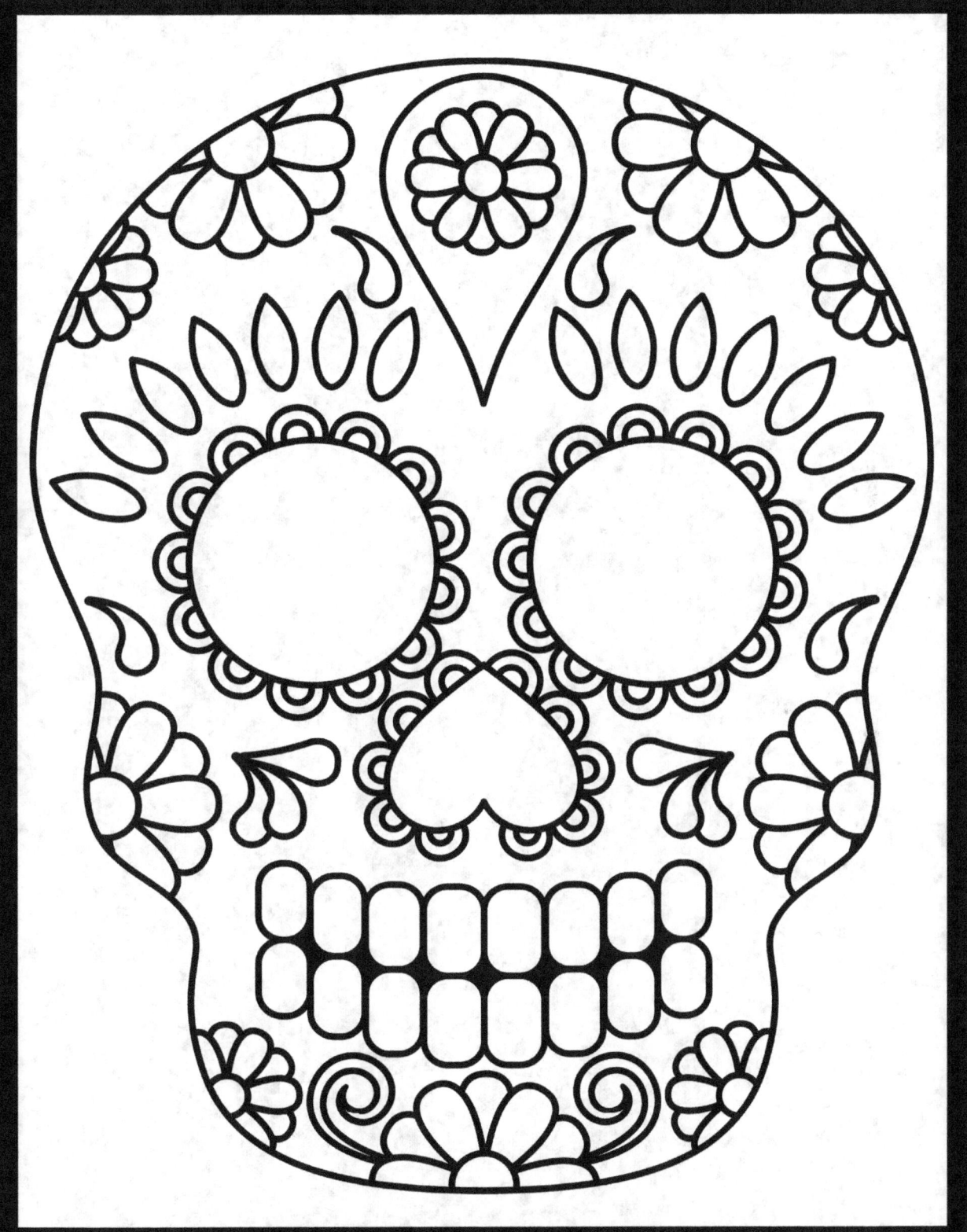

Sugar Skull 21
BONJOUR PRINTABLES

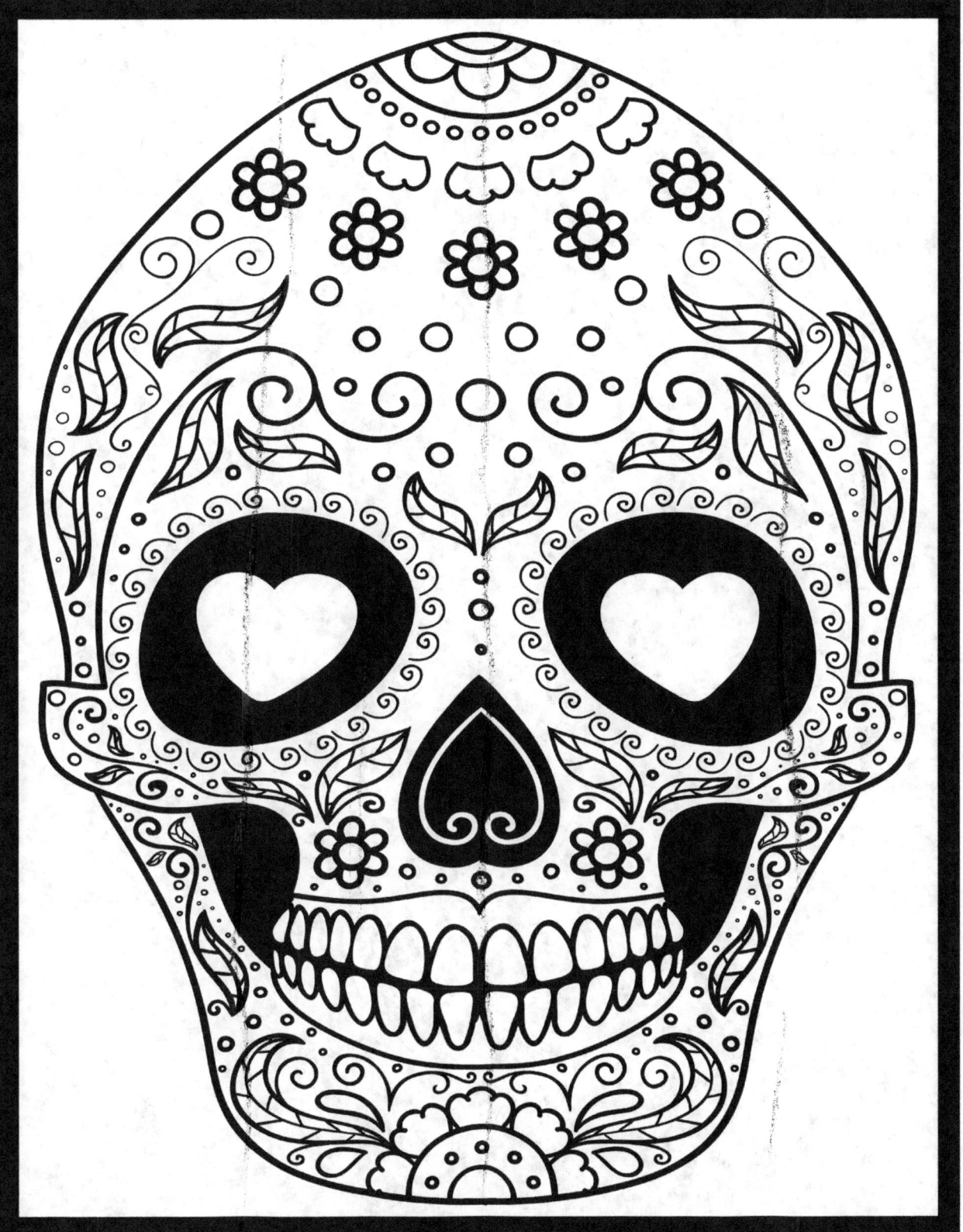

Sugar Skull 22
BONJOUR PRINTABLES

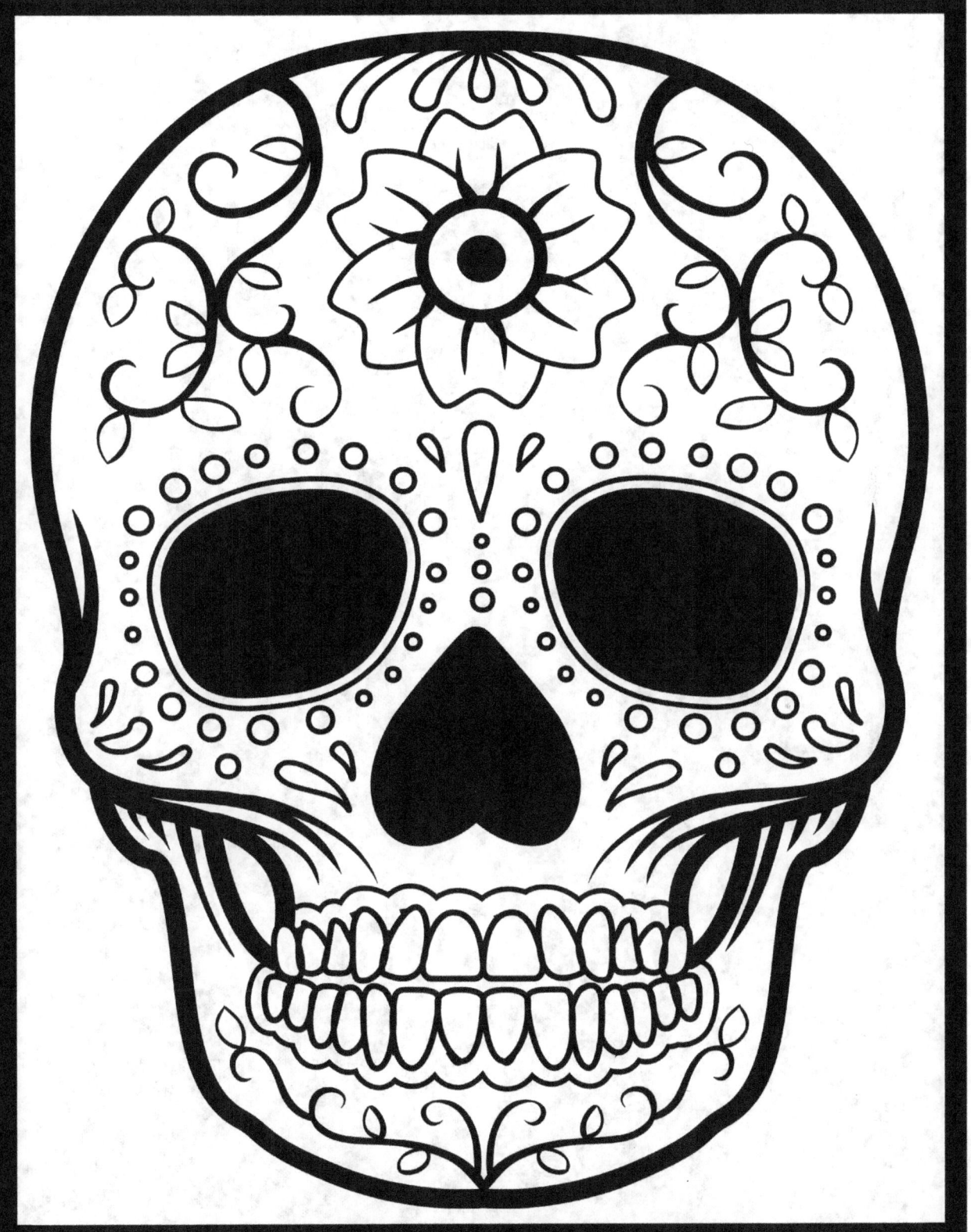

Sugar Skull 23
BONJOUR PRINTABLES

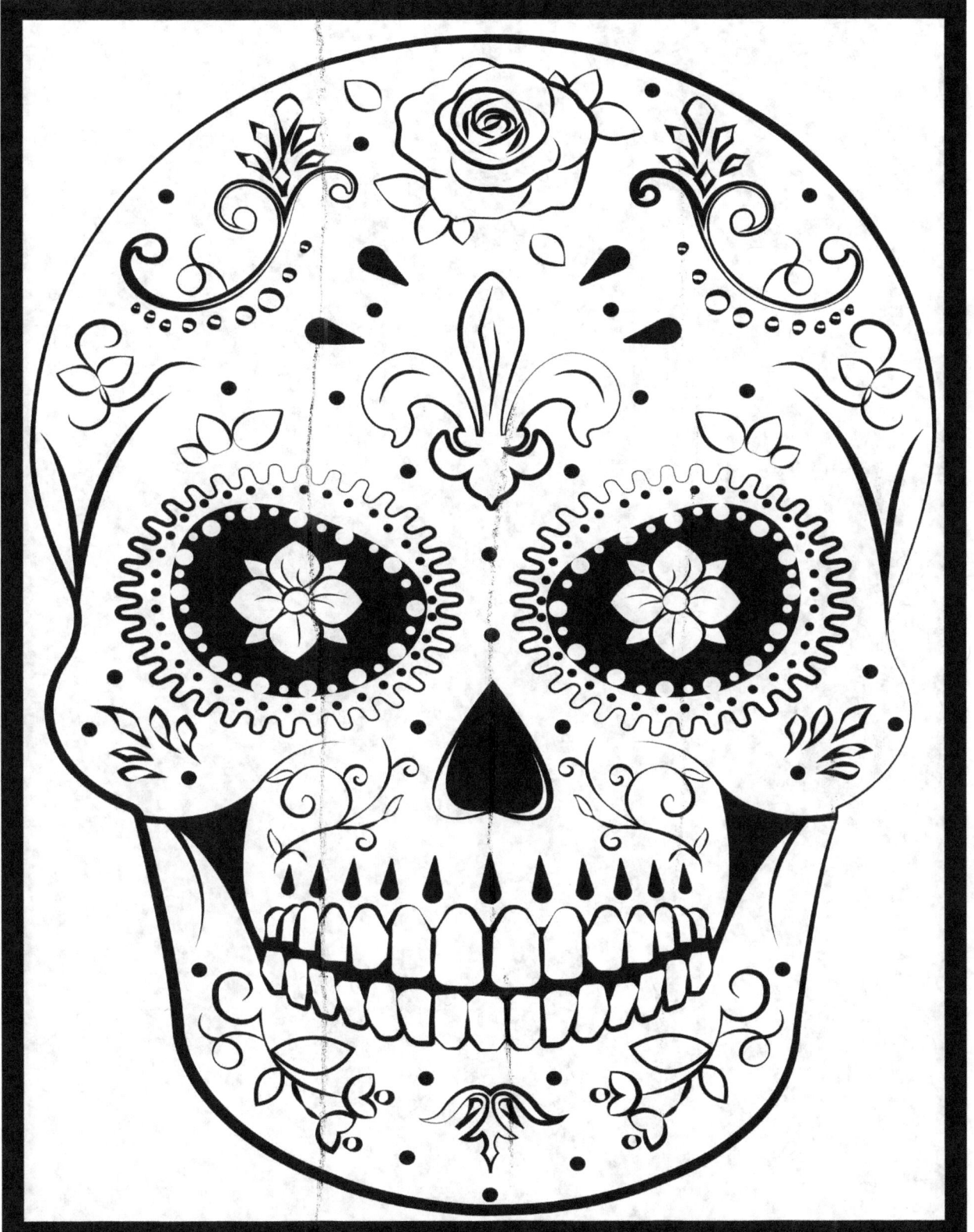

Sugar skull 24
BONJOUR PRINTABLES

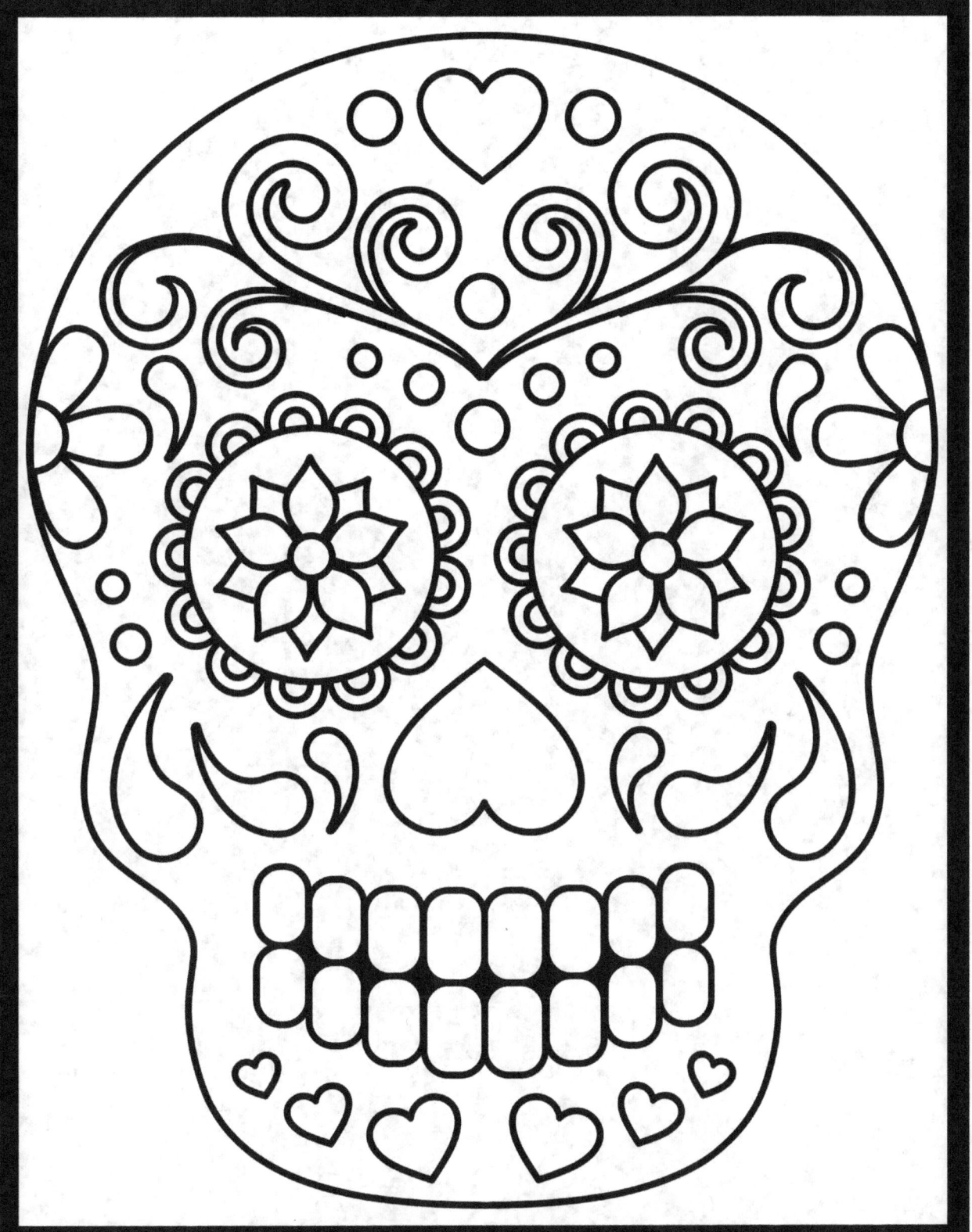

Sugar Skull 25
BONJOUR PRINTABLES

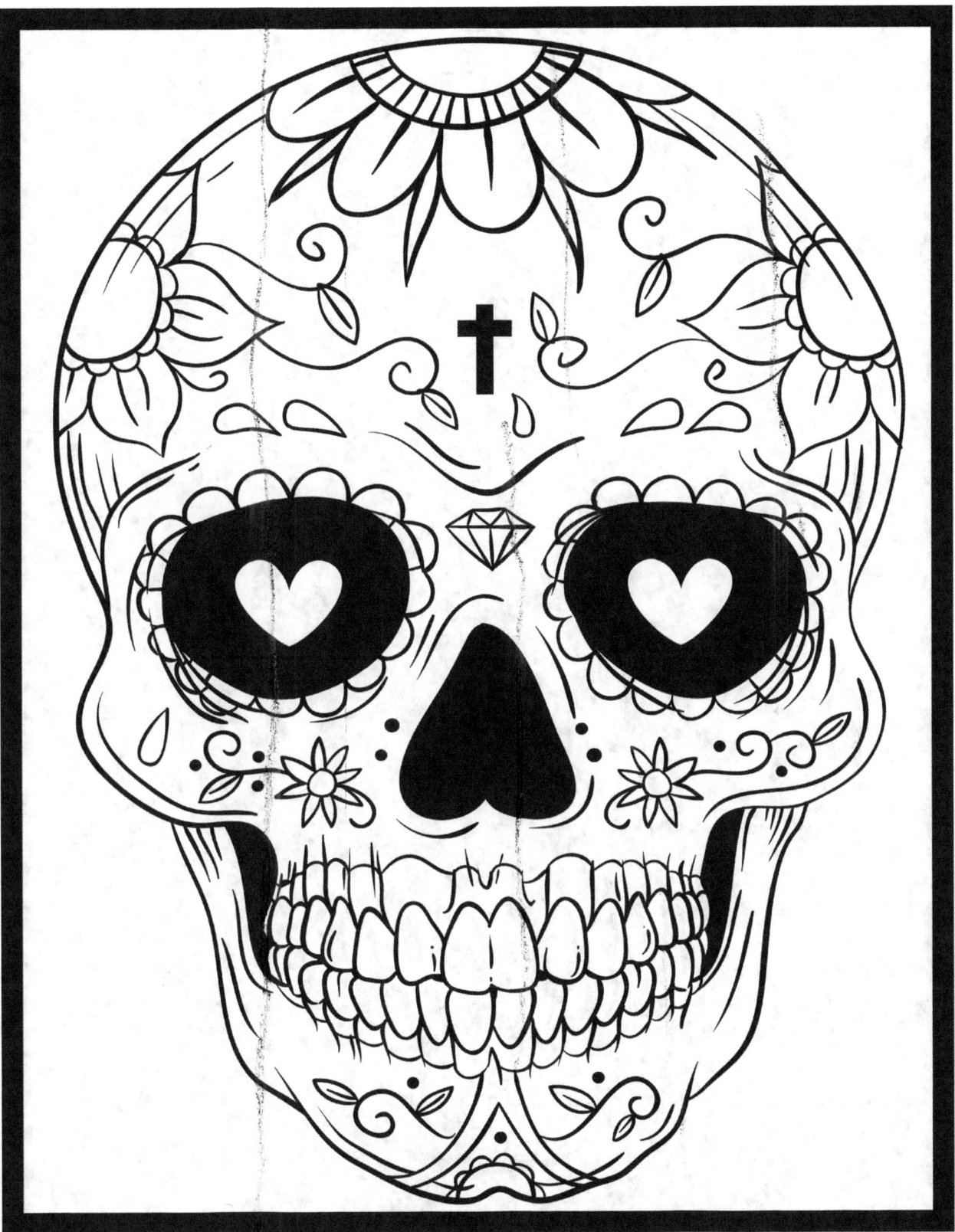

Sugar Skull 26

BONJOUR PRINTABLES

www.ingramcontent.com/pod-product-compliance
Lightning Source LLC
Chambersburg PA
CBHW080952220526
45465CB00008BA/3259